GW00786422

WEL
Wit & Humour

CAMILLA ZAJAC

BRADWELL
BOOKS

Published by Bradwell Books
9 Orgreave Close Sheffield S13 9NP
Email: books@bradwellbooks.co.uk

Complied by Camilla Zajac

British Library Cataloguing in Publication Data: a catalogue record for this
book is available
from the British Library.

1st Edition
ISBN: 9781902674599

Print: Gomer Press, Llandysul, Ceredigion SA44 4JL
Design by: JenksDesign
Illustrations: ©Tim O'Brien 2013

An Englishman, Irishman, Welshman and Scotsman were captured while fighting in a foreign land, and the leader of the captors said, 'We're going to line you up in front of a firing squad and shoot you all in turn. But first, you each can make a final wish.'

The Englishman responds, 'I'd like to hear 'God Save The Queen' just one more time to remind me of the auld country, played by the London All Boys Choir. With Morris Dancers Dancing to the tune.'

The Irishman replies, 'I'd like to hear 'Danny Boy' just one more time to remind me of the auld country, sung in the style of Daniel O'Donnell, with Riverdance dancers skipping gaily to the tune.'

The Welshman answers, 'I'd like to hear "Men Of Harlech" just one more time to remind me of the country, sung as if by the Treorchy Male Voice Choir.'

The Scotsman says quickly, 'I'd like to be shot first.'

What do you call an Englishman holding a bottle of champagne after a Six Nations game?

Waiter.

What do you call a Welshman with no brain?

Dim.

A man walks into a bookshop and says 'I hope you don't have a book on reverse psychology.'

An English politician was giving a speech in Aberystwyth. He said: 'I was born an Englishman. I have been an Englishman all my life, and I will die an Englishman!'

'What's wrong, boyo?' shouted a voice from the crowd. 'Got no ambition, have you?'.

Rhys: 'Doctor, I can't stop singing the Green, Green Grass of Home.'

Doctor: 'That sounds like Tom Jones syndrome.'

Rhys: 'Is it common?'

Doctor: 'It's not unusual.'

What do you get if you cross the Welsh Rugby Union with an OXO cube?

A laughing stock.

What did the cheese salesman say?

'That cheese may be Gouda, but this one is Feta!'

Did you hear about the two men from the monastery who opened up a seafood restaurant? One was the fish friar, and the other was the chip monk.

A farmer was out on his Welsh hillside tending his flock one day, when he saw a man drinking with a cupped hand from the stream which ran down from one of his fields. Realising the danger, he shouted over to the man, 'Paid a yfed y dwr! Mae'n ych-y-fi!' [Don't drink the water. It's disgusting!]

The man at the stream lifted his head and put a cupped hand to his ear, shrugged his shoulders at the farmer, and carried on drinking.

Realising the man at the stream couldn't hear him, the farmer moved closer, 'Paid a yfed! Dwr ych-y-fi! Defaid yn cachu yn y dwr!' [Don't drink. Water's disgusting. Sheep dung in the water.]

Still the walker couldn't hear the farmer. Finally the farmer walked right up to the man at the stream and once again said again, 'Dwr yn ych-y-fi! Paid a'i yfed!'. [Water's disgusting. Don't drink it!]

'I'm dreadfully sorry my good man, I can't understand a word you say dear boy! Can't you speak English?' Said the man at the stream, in a splendid English accent.

'Oh I see', said the farmer, 'I was just saying, if you use both hands you can get more in!

Did you hear that they've crossed a Newfoundland and a Basset Hound? The new breed is a Newfound Asset Hound, a dog for financial advisors.

What gets wetter and wetter the more it dries?

A towel.

Mrs Hopkins ordered a shoulder of Welsh lamb from her butcher, Mr Davies. She suspected that the meat she had been given was not the genuine article.

'Are you certain this is real Welsh lamb?' Mrs Hopkins demanded, angrily.

'Ah, well, Mrs Hopkins,' confessed Mr Davies, the butcher. 'Look you, that lamb was actually born in New Zealand, but I can assure you that it had Welsh parents.'

What goes around the world but stays in a corner?

A stamp.

How many surrealists does it take to screw in a lightbulb?

Banana.

Did you hear that they've crossed a Newfoundland and a Basset Hound? The new breed is a Newfound Asset Hound, a dog for financial advisors.

I have holes in my top and bottom, my left and right and in the middle. What am I?

A sponge.

Three Englishmen walk into a bar and spot a Welshman sitting alone at a table.

One fellow said to the others, 'Let's pick a fight with that Welshman over there.'

His partner replied, 'Wait, we don't want to be arrested. Let's make him start the fight.'

The third Englishman said, 'Wait here chaps. I know how to do it.'

He went over to the Welshman and said, 'St David was a flippin' sissy.'

To this the Welshman replied, 'Ah well, you don't say!' and calmly resumed drinking his beer.

The second Englishman now tried his luck and said to the Welshman, 'St David was a stupid fool that wore a dress!'

The Welshman again replied, 'You're very sharp, you don't say!' and calmly resumed drinking his beer.

The last Englishman told his friends he knew how to rile the Welshman and bounced up to the table and yelled, 'St David was an Englishman!'

The Welshman replied, calmly, 'That's what your mates were trying to tell me.'

A group of chess enthusiasts checked into a hotel and were standing in reception discussing their recent tournament victories. After about an hour, the manager came out of the office and asked them to move. 'But why?' they asked, as they walked off. 'Because,' he said 'I can't stand chess nuts boasting in an open foyer.'

A young boy was describing in an essay his holiday in Aberystwyth, he astonished and delighted his teacher by spelling the town's name correctly every time he used it.

The next, day Miss Jones, his teacher called him to the front of the class and said 'Show the class how well you can spell. Write 'Aberystwyth' on the blackboard.'

'Please, Miss Jones, I can't any more,' Morgan pleaded, 'I've eaten all my rock.'

I went into the woods and got it. I sat down to seek it. I brought it home with me because I couldn't find it. What is it?

A splinter.

Two men, Cadwaladr and Dewi shared an old two-roomed farmhouse somewhere west of Llanfarian. Cadwaladr grumbled to a visitor, 'Dewi makes life unbearable at times. He keeps sheep and goats in the bedroom and it smells terrible.'

'Why don't you open the window?' came the reply.

'What, and let all my pigeons escape?'.

What is the longest word in the English language?

Smiles. Because there is a mile between its first and last letters.

I went to Cardiff last week and had a run in with the Taffia, the Welsh contingent of the Mafia.

They made me an offer I couldn't understand.

What do you do if you are driving your car in Cardiff and you see a spaceman?

Park in it, of course.

Ianto was having a pint at his local when a very loud mouthed Englishman called Henry walked in. Ianto couldn't help overhearing Henry trying to bet a couple of young lads that they couldn't drink 20 pints in 20 minutes. After a lot of cajoling, Henry was unsuccessful in his goal to make a few quid. He looked around at Ianto and said 'Well what about you then?, Are you game?' Ianto downed his pint and left the pub.

Half an hour later Ianto walked back into his local and said to Henry 'I'll take that bet.'

Sure enough Henry smiled at the easy money he would make as Ianto began to drink the pints. Henry's smile soon disappeared when Ianto polished off the 20 pints in 19 minutes. Handing over the cash, Henry said 'When you left the here earlier, where did you go?' Ianto looked at him and replied 'I had to go to the pub down the road to see if I could do it first.'

Two snowmen are standing in a field. One says to the other 'That's funny, I can smell carrots.'

Why do seagulls live by the sea?

Because if they lived by the bay they would be called bagels.

Why was the scarecrow promoted?

He was outstanding in his field!

Have you heard about the latest machine on the pier at Llandudno?

You put ten pence in and ask it any question and it gives you a true answer.

One holiday maker from Cardiff tried it last week.

He asked the machine 'Where is my father?' The machine replied:

'Your father is fishing in South Wales.'

Well, he thought, that's daft for a start because my father is dead.

'Where is my mother's husband?'

Back came the reply, 'Your mother's husband is buried in Cardiff but your father is still fishing in South Wales.'

What's green and runs around the garden?

A hedge.

How do you know if you're a pirate or not?.

You just know you arrrrrhh.

I'm part of the bird that's not in the sky. I can swim in the ocean and yet remain dry. What am I?

A shadow.

A Russian spy was dropped by parachute in the Welsh hills with instructions to contact a Mr Jones who lived in the small village of Llanfair, and give him the code message 'The tulips are blooming well today.'

Arriving at the village, he asked a small boy where Mr Jones lived and was directed to a small cottage at the end of the village.

He knocked on the door and the owner emerged. 'Are you Mr Jones?'

'I am.'

'The tulips are blooming well today.'

Mr. Jones stared at him in amazement and then smiled.

'Ah, you must have come to the wrong house. It's Jones-the-spy you want.'

Letter from Welsh Lodging-House Keeper:

'I should like to know, please, whether you want two bedrooms with double beds in them, or two double-bedded rooms, as I have only one double-bedded room; all the beds are double beds except one in the double-bedded room, which is a single bed.'

Did you hear about the man who was convicted of stealing luggage from the airport?

He asked for twenty other cases to be taken into account.

They say an Englishman laughs three times at a joke. The first time when everybody gets it, the second a week later when he thinks he gets it, the third time a month later when somebody explains it to him.

Two boys were arguing when the teacher entered the room.

The teacher says, 'Why are you arguing?'

One boy answers, 'We found a ten pound note and decided to give it to whoever tells the biggest lie.

'You should be ashamed of yourselves,' said the teacher, 'When I was your age I didn't even know what a lie was.'

The boys gave the ten pound note to the teacher.

A life-long city man, tired of the rat race in his home town of Cardiff, decided he was going to give up the city life, move to the country, and become a chicken farmer. He bought a nice organic chicken farm in the Vale of Glamorgan and moved in. It turned out that his next door neighbour was also a chicken farmer. A neighbour came for a visit one day and said, 'Chicken farming isn't easy. So, to help you get started, I'll give you 100 chickens.'

The new chicken farmer was delighted. Two weeks later the neighbour dropped by to see how things were going. The new farmer said, 'Not too well mate. All 100 chickens died.' The neighbour said, 'Oh, I can't believe that. I've never had any trouble with my chickens. I'll give you 100 more.' Another two weeks went by and the neighbour dropped in again. The new farmer said, 'You're not going to believe this, but the second 100 chickens died too.' Astounded, the neighbour asked, 'What went wrong?'

The new farmer said, 'Well, I'm not sure whether I'm planting them too deep or too close together.'

A man wanted to become a monk so he went to the monastery and talked to the head monk.

The head monk said, 'You must take a vow of silence and can only say two words every three years.'

The man agreed and after the first three years, the head monk came to him and said, 'What are your two words?'

'Food cold!' the man replied.

Three more years went by and the head monk came to him and said 'What are your two words?'

'Robe dirty!' the man exclaimed.

Three more years went by and the head monk came to him and said, 'What are your two words?'

'I quit!' said the man.

'Well', the head monk replied, 'I'm not surprised. You've done nothing but complain ever since you got here!'

Two men who arrived late at a crowded theatre in Cardiff could not find a seat and had to stand at the back.

Getting tired after the first act, one of them shouted loudly at the beginning of the interval

'Mr. Evans's house is on fire.'

They immediately had the choice of nineteen vacant seats.

I never was, am always to be.
No one ever saw me, nor ever will.
And yet I am the confidence of all
To live and breathe on this terrestrial ball.
What am I?

Tomorrow.

A duck walks into a pub and goes up to the barman.

The barman says 'What can I get you?'

Duck: 'Umm. Do you have any grapes?'

Barman (Looking surprised):

'No, I'm afraid we don't.'

The duck waddles slowly out of the pub.

The next day at the same time, the duck waddles into the pub, hops up on a bar stool.

Barman: 'Hi. What can I get for you?'

Duck: 'Um. Do you have any grapes?'

Barman (a little annoyed): 'Hey! Weren't you in here yesterday. Look mate, we don't have any grapes. OK?'

The duck hops off the stool and waddles out of the door.

The next day, at the same time, the barman is cleaning some glasses when he hears a familiar voice

Duck: 'Umm... Do you have any grapes?'

The barman is really annoyed

Barman: 'Look. What's your problem? You came in here yesterday asking for grapes, I told you, we don't have any grapes! Next time I see your little ducktail waddle in here I'm going to nail those little webbed feet of yours to the floor. GOT me pal?'

So the duck hops off the bar stool and waddles out.

The next day at the same time, the duck waddles into the pub, walks up to the barman and the barman says,

'What on earth do YOU want?'

'Errrr. do you have any nails?'

'What!? Of course not.'

'Oh. Well, do you have any grapes?'

Special names from Wales:

The man with only two teeth left and those in the front of his mouth - Dai central eating

After H.G. Wells discovered that Oliver Cromwell's real name was Williams and that his ancestors came from Margam, he always referred to him as "Williams-the-Conqueror".

The local chiropodist - Williams the corn-curer.

A Welsh physicist - Dai-atomic.

A reckless risk-taker - Huw ap Hazard.

A new client had just come in to see a famous lawyer.

'Can you tell me how much you charge?', said the client.

'Of course', the lawyer replied, 'I charge £200 to answer three questions!'

'Well that's a bit steep, isn't it?'

'Yes it is,' said the lawyer, 'And what's your third question?'

From the beginning of eternity
To the end of time and space
To the beginning of every end
And the end of every place.
What am I?

The letter 'e'.

Three Welshmen in a pub praising the beer:

First Welshman: 'Best glass of beer I never tasted no better.'

Second Welshman: 'So did I neither.'

Third Welshman: 'Neither did I too.

All about, but cannot be seen.

Can be captured, cannot be held.

No throat, but can be heard.

What is it?

The wind.

Sam works in an office in Swansea, he went into his boss's office. He said to him

'I'll be honest with you, I know the economy isn't great, but I have three companies after me, and I would like to respectfully ask for a pay rise.'

After a few minutes of haggling his manager finally agrees to a 5% raise, and Sam happily gets up to leave.

'By the way', asks the boss as Sam is getting up, 'Which three companies are after you?'

'The electric company, the water company, and the phone company', Sam replies.

Notice outside London theatre: 'The part of the Welshman has been filled. The Dai is cast.'

Language student to teacher, 'Are 'trousers' singular or plural?'
Teacher, 'They're singular on top and plural on the bottom.'

Why was the computer so tired when it got home?
Because it had a hard drive!

What kind of ears does an engine have?

Engineers.

A visitor to Llanrwst asked a local resident to direct him to the house of Mr. Evan Griffiths. The reply was: 'You see those two houses at the top of the hill? Well, Mr. Griffiths lives in the middle one.'

What do you get when you cross a dog with a telephone?

A Golden Receiver!

What do cats like to eat for breakfast?

Mice Krispies

What goes round the house and in the house but never touches the house?

The sun.

Tourist in Barmouth: 'Have you got anything in the shape of motor car tyres?' Shopkeeper: 'Oh, yes. We've got lifebuoys, invalid cushions, funeral wreaths and doughnuts.'

If you ever wondered where all the Davies come from, there's a big factory outside Bridgend with a sign outside saying 'Davies Manufacturing Co. Ltd.'

Though it is not an ox, it has horns; though it is not an ass, it has a pack-saddle; and wherever it goes it leaves silver behind. What is it?

A snail.

A little old lady in Tenby earned her living by selling tea and cakes to trippers from England.

Being the daughter of a mean old South Gower farmer, she tried to boost her profits by using the same tea bags over and over again.

At first no one noticed and she made a lot of money.

The word got around that her tea wasn't what it used to be, the trippers stopped coming and she went out of business.

Moral: Honest tea is the best policy.

He who has it doesn't tell it. He who takes it doesn't know it. He who knows it doesn't want it. What is it?

Counterfeit money.

It is now many years since the last train stopped at the railway station with the longest name in Britain Llanfairpwllgwyngyllgogerychwyrndrobwll - Llantysilio - gogogoch in Anglesey.

When a train stopped at the station the porter would cry out 'Anybody in there for here?'

An Englishman went into a hardware store and asked to buy a sink.

'Would you like one with a plug?' asked the assistant.

'Don't tell me they've gone electric,' said the Englishman.

Two aerials meet on a roof - fall in love - get married. The ceremony was rubbish - but the reception was brilliant.

A little old lady, visiting the seaside at Conwy for the first time, saw some men preparing to go fishing, collecting their baskets and nets.

She said to one of them: 'What are those things?'

He said 'Lobster pots.'

She said 'Go on, you'll never train them to sit on those things!'

Why couldn't Cinderella be a good soccer player?

She lost her shoe, she ran away from the ball, and her coach was a pumpkin.

What do you call a boomerang that won't come back?

A stick.

The Reverend Huw Jones, a Minister from Wales, was travelling home one night and was greatly annoyed when a young man, much the worse for drink, came and sat next to him on the bus.

'Young man,' the Minister, declared in a rather pompous tone, 'Do you not realise you are on the road to perdition?'

'Oh, hell and botheration,' retorted the drunkard, 'I could have sworn this bus went to Llanelli.'

A man enters a dark cabin. He has just one match with him. There is an oil lamp, a wood stove, and a fireplace in the cabin. What would he light first?

The match.

After having dug to a depth of 10 meters last year, Scottish scientists found traces of copper wire dating back 100 years and came to the conclusion that their ancestors already had a telephone network more than 100 years ago.

Not to be outdone by the Scots, in the weeks that followed, English scientists dug to a depth of 20 metres, and shortly after, headlines in the London newspapers read: 'English archaeologists have found traces of 200 year old copper wire and have concluded that their ancestors already had an advanced high-tech communications network a hundred years earlier than the Scots.'

One week later, a Welsh newspaper, reported the following: 'After digging as deep as 30 metres in a peat bog near Tonypandy, Dai 'Digger' Davies, a self-taught archaeologist and eminent worrier of sheep, reported that he found absolutely nothing. It has therefore been concluded that, 300 years ago, Wales had already gone wireless.'

A Welsh fan was watching a Six Nations game against Ireland in Dublin.

In the packed stadium, there was only one empty seat - right next to him.

'Who does that seat belong to?' asked Dai from the row behind.

'I got the ticket for my wife,' replied the fan

'But why isn't she here?

'I'm afraid she died in an accident.'

'So you're keeping the seat vacant as a mark of respect,' said Dai.

'No,' said the fan, 'I offered it to all of my friends.'

'So why didn't they take it,' asked a puzzled Dai.

'They've all gone to the funeral.'

A father and his son, Bobby, arrive at the local Rugby match in Wales and Dad can't find the tickets. Dad: 'Nip home and see if I left the tickets there.' Bobby: 'No probs, Dad.' Half an hour later Bobby returns to his dad who is patiently waiting outside the stadium. Bobby: 'Yep, they're on the kitchen table where you left them.'

What gear were you in at the moment of the impact?

Gucci sweats and Reeboks.

How do you make a sausage roll?

Push it!

A man went to the doctor one day and said: 'I've just been playing Rugby and when I got back I found that when I touched my legs, my arms, my head, my tummy and everywhere else, it really hurt.' So the doctor said: 'Yes, that's because you've broken your finger.'

What do the Ospreys and a three pin electrical plug have in common?

They're both useless in Europe.

Your mother's brother's only brother-in-law is your Stepfather, Grandfather, Uncle or Father?

Your Father.

Three tourists were driving through Wales. As they were approaching Llanfairpwllgwyngyllgogerychwyrndrobwllllantysiliogogogoch, they started arguing about the pronunciation of the town's name. They argued back and forth until they stopped for lunch. As they stood at the counter one asked the employee, 'Before we order, could you please settle an argument for us? Would you please pronounce where we are... very slowly?' The girl leaned over the counter and said, 'Burrrrrr, gerrrrrr, Kiiiiiing.'

"Brothers and sisters have I none, yet that man's father is my father's son" who is "that man"?

That man is your son.

A Cambrian farmer's dog goes missing and he is inconsolable.

His wife says to him, 'Why don't you put an ad in the paper to get him back?'

The farmer does this, but after two weeks, no phone calls, the dog is still missing.

'What did you write in the paper?' asked his wife.

'Here boy,' said the farmer.

My life can be measured in hours;
I serve by being devoured.
Thin, I am quick; fat, I am slow.
Wind is my foe.
What am I?

A candle.

A teacher at a High School was having a little trouble getting her year 11 pupils to understand grammar, 'These are what we call the pronouns', she said, 'And the way we use them with verbs; I am, you are, he/she is' she was saying, to glazed looks.

Trying a different tack she said, 'Johnny, give me a sentence with the pronoun, 'I' in it.'

Dai began, 'I is...'

'No, no, no, no, no NO, NO!', shouted the teacher, 'Never, 'I is', always, 'I am'... now try again'.

Dai looked puzzled and a little hurt, thought a while then began again more quietly,'I... am...the ninth letter of the alphabet'.

What does one star say to another star when they meet?

Glad to meteor!

An Englishman was walking down the street in Llandudno when he met Pit Davies standing beside a big strong horse.

'How much do you want for this horse?' asked the Englishman.

Pit answered, 'This horse doesn't look good these days.'

The Englishman said, 'I've been trading horses all my life and there's nothing a country boy like you can tell me about them. Just name your price and let me be the judge of what's good-looking and what's not.'

'Two thousand pounds,' said Pit.

'Deal,' said the Englishman and bought the horse. When he was leading the horse, it walked right into a lamppost. The Englishman ran back to Pit and shouted,

'You didn't tell me the horse was blind!'

Pit said, 'But I told you this horse didn't look good.'

A passenger in a taxi tapped the driver on the shoulder to ask him something.

The driver screamed, lost control of the cab, nearly hit a bus, drove up over the curb and stopped just inches from a large plate glass window.

For a few moments everything was silent in the cab, then the driver said, 'Please, don't ever do that again. You scared the daylights out of me.'

The passenger, who was also frightened, apologised and said he didn't

realize that a tap on the shoulder could frighten him so much, to which the

driver replied, 'I'm sorry, it's really not your fault at all. Today is my

first day driving a cab. I've been driving a hearse for the last 25 years.'

What lies at the bottom of the ocean and twitches?

A nervous wreck.

How do you approach an angry Welsh cheese?

Caerphilly.

A man walks into a doctor's office with two onions under his arms, a potato in his ear and a carrot up his nose. He asks the doctor: 'What's wrong with me?'

The doctor replies: 'You're not eating properly.'

What's the difference between roast beef and pea soup?

Anyone can roast beef.

What time does Sean Connery arrive at Wimbledon?

Tennish.

An Englishman, a Welshman and an Irishman were at the fair and about to go on the helter-skelter when an old crone stepped in front of them.

'This is a magic ride,' she said. 'You will land in whatever you shout out on the way down.'

'I'm game for this,' said the Welshman and slides down the helter-skelter shouting 'GOLD!' at the top of his voice. Sure enough, when he hit the bottom he found himself surrounded by thousands of pounds worth of gold coins.

The Englishman goes next and shouts 'SILVER!' at the top of his voice. At the bottom he lands in more silver coinage than he can carry.

The Irishman goes last and, launching himself from the top of the slide shouts 'WEEEEEEE!'.

Why is 6 afraid of 7?

Because 7, 8, 9!

What do you give a sick budgie?

Tweetment.

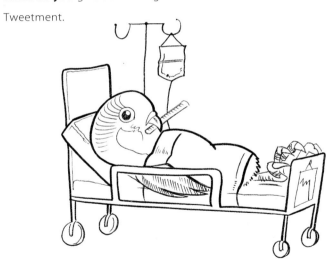

What do you call a hippie's wife?

Mississippi.

You can have me but cannot hold me;
Gain me and quickly lose me.
If treated with care I can be great,
And if betrayed I will break.
What am I?

Trust.

An Englishman, an Irishman and a Scotsman walk into a bar.

The Barman says 'Is this a joke?'

Where do generals keep their armies?

Up their sleevies.

What do you get if you cross a nun and a chicken?

A pecking order!

My thunder comes before the lightning:

My lightning comes before the clouds:

My rain dries all the land it touches.

What am I?

A volcano.

What kind of coat can only be put on when wet?

A coat of paint.

Five Englishmen boarded a train just behind five Welshmen, who, as a group had only purchased one ticket. Just before the conductor came through, all the Welshmen piled into the toilet stall at the back of the car.

As the conductor passed the stall, he knocked and called 'Tickets, please!' and one of the Welshmen slid a ticket under the door. It was punched, pushed back under the door, and when it was safe all the Welshmen came out and took their seats.

The Englishmen were tremendously impressed by this ingenuity. On the trip back, the five Englishmen decided to try this themselves and purchased only one ticket. They noticed that, oddly, the Welshmen had not purchased any tickets this time.

Anyway, again, just before the conductor came through, the Welshmen piled into one of the toilet stalls, the Englishmen into the other. Then one of the Welshmen leaned out, knocked on the Englishmen's stall and called 'Ticket, please!' When the ticket slid out under the door, he picked it up and quickly closed the door.

Four men sat down to play.
and played all night till break of day.
They played for gold and not for fun.
with separate scores for every one.
Yet when they came to square accounts.
they all had made quite fair amounts!
Can you the paradox explain?
If no one lost. how could all gain?

The four men were all fiddlers in a band and were each paid £5 at the end of the night. It is tempting to assume that they were playing cards, but that is not stated!

I am seen in places that appear to need me not.

I come seldom to places that need me most.

Sometimes my arrival is celebrated,

at others times I am hated.

I refresh all things whether they need it or not.

Rain.

Who succeeded the first Prime Minister?

The second one!

56

One day, an Englishman, a Scotsman, and a Welshman walked into a pub together. They each bought a pint of Guinness.

Just as they were about to enjoy their drinks, three flies landed in each of their pints, and were stuck in the thick head. The Englishman pushed his beer away in disgust. The Scotsman fished the fly out of his beer, and continued drinking it, as if nothing had happened.

The Welshman, too, picked the fly out of his drink, held it out over the beer, and started yelling "Spit it out! Spit it out now!".

What did Geronimo shout when he jumped out of the aeroplane?

ME!

I am so small, and sometimes I'm missed.

I get misplaced, misused, and help you when you list.

People usually pause when they see me.

So can you tell me what I could be?

A comma.

What has five eyes, but cannot see?

The Mississippi River.

What has a head like a cat, feet like a cat, a tail like a cat, but isn't a cat?

A kitten.

Light as a feather,

Nothing in it.

Few can hold it,

For even a minute.

Your breath.

The Pope is visiting Wales and while viewing the coastline he looks out to sea where two Welsh Rugby fans are out in a boat, suddenly in the water he sees an English rugby fan being attacked by a shark. Immediately the boat arrives on the scene, the Welsh fans drag the English fan into the boat, kill the shark with a knife and haul it into the boat.

The Pope seeing this beckons the boat into the shore and says 'I have never seen anything so brave, I understood that there was animosity between English and Welsh rugby fans but that has restored my faith in mankind'. He then blesses the Welshmen and departs without another word.

The one guy turns to his mate and says 'What was he on about?'

'Dunno' says his mate 'He knows sod all about fishing. Do we need any fresh bait?'

The old king is dying, and wants to leave his kingdom to the wiser of his two sons. He tells them that he will hold a horse-race, and the son whose horse is the last to reach the bridge and come back will inherit the realm. Immediately the younger son jumps on a horse and makes for the bridge at top speed. The king now knows that this is the wiser son, and leaves him the kingdom. Why?

The younger son jumped on the older son's horse. He realized that if they rode their own horses the race would never end.

I do not breathe, but I run and jump.

I do not eat, but I swim and stretch.

I do not drink, but I sleep and stand.

I do not think, but I grow and play.

I do not see, but you see me every day.

I am a leg.

What was given to you, belongs to you exclusively and yet is used more by your friends than by yourself?

Your name.

Unusual Welsh place names

Aberflyarf

Fiddler's Elbow

Golly

Kemeys Commander

Llanfairpwllgwyngyllgogerychwyrndrobwyllllantysiliogogogoch

Mold

Pant

Plwmp

Splott

Stop-and-Call

If it's not the day after Monday or the day before Thursday, and it isn't Sunday tomorrow, and it wasn't Sunday yesterday, and the day after tomorrow isn't Saturday, and the day before yesterday wasn't Wednesday, what day is it?

Sunday.

How many cats are in a small room if in each of the four corners a cat is sitting, and opposite each cat there sit three cats, and at each cat's tail a cat is sitting?

Four cats - each near the tail of the cat in the adjacent corner (it's a small room!)

The Welsh team were playing England at Twickenham and after the half-time whistle blew they found themselves ahead 50-0, Neil Jenkins getting eight tries. The rest of the team decided to head for the pub instead of playing the second half, leaving Neil to go out on his own.

'No worries,' Neil told them, 'I'll join you later and tell you what happened.' After the game Neil headed for the pub where he told his team-mates the final score: 95-3.

'What!' said a furious team mate, 'How did you let them get three points?' Neil replied apologetically, 'I was sent off with 20 minutes to go.'

A girl who was just learning to drive went down a one-way street in the wrong direction, but didn't break the law. How come?

She was walking.

A man builds a house rectangular in shape. All the sides have southern exposure. A big bear walks by. What colour is the bear? Why?

The bear is white because the house is built on the North Pole.

The club president, coach, a prop and a wing are taking a charter flight to the National Rugby Finals when the engines cut out. The pilot enters the passenger compartment and says, 'We're going down. There's only four parachutes! Since I'm the pilot I'm taking one,' and then jumps from the plane.

The coach says, 'Without me, the team won't have a chance, so I'm taking one,' and he jumps out. The winger says, 'I'm the fastest and smartest man on the pitch and without me the team can't win a game, so I'm taking one,' and he jumps out of the plane.

The club president looks at the prop and says, 'You take the last parachute. The team needs you more than it needs me'. The prop responds, 'We can both take a parachute. The smartest man on the pitch just jumped out of the plane with my kit bag on his back.'

What starts with a 'P', ends with an 'E' and has thousands of letters?

The Post Office!

What, when you need it you throw it away, but when you don't need it you take it back?

An anchor.

What jumps when it walks and sits when it stands?

A kangaroo.

Two Welshmen, Dylan and Glyn, are sitting on a park bench reading their newspapers.

Dylan notices the headline, '12 Brazilian Soldiers Killed.'

Turning to Glyn, Dylan enquires, 'Just how many is a Brazilian?'

What is it that you can keep after giving it to someone else?

Your word

A Welshman goes up to the bar, says to his friend, Dai, 'Do you want to hear a 'blond' joke?',

On overhearing this, two large blond lady wrestlers strode up to him, demanding to hear his blond joke.

'O'eer I've forgotten it', says the Welshman

'Scared you did they?', says Dai.

'No I couldn't be bothered to explain it twice', says his friend.

A box without hinges, key, or lid, Yet golden treasure inside is hid. What is it?

An egg.

The more you take, the more you leave behind. What are they?

Footsteps.

What walks all day on its head?

A nail in a horse shoe.

In the beginning, God turned to the archangel Gabriel and said 'Today I am going to create a beautiful part of the earth and call it Wales. I will make a country of breath-taking blue lakes rich green forests and dark beautiful mountains which from time to time will be snow covered. I will give it clear swift rivers which will overflow with salmon and trout.

The land shall be lush and fertile on which the people can raise cattle and grow their food as well as being rich with precious metals and stones which will be much sought after the world over. Underneath the land I shall lay rich seams of coal for the inhabitants to mine. Around the coast I will make some of the most beautiful areas in the world. White sandy beaches and cliffs that will attract all manner of wildlife, and lots of islands that will be like paradise to all that visit them.

In the waters around the shores there will be an abundance of sea life. The people who live there shall be called the Welsh and will be the friendliest on the earth.'

'Excuse me sire' interrupted the archangel Gabriel, 'Don't you think you are being a bit generous to the people of Wales?'

'Don't talk rubbish' replied the Lord, 'Wait till you see the neighbours I'm giving them!'

Harry proudly drove his new convertible into town and parked it on the main street, he was on his way to the recycle centre to get rid of an unwanted gift, a foot spa, which he left on the back seat.

He had walked half way down the street when he realised that he had left the top down... with the foot spa in the back.

He ran all the way back to his car, but it was too late...

Another five foot spas had been dumped in the car.